GRATITUDE JOURNAL FOR TEENS

PROMPTS TO CULTIVATE A HABIT OF AWARENESS AND IMPROVE WELL-BEING

SCARLET PAOLICCHI

ROCKRIDGE
PRESS

Interior and Cover Designer: Karmen Lizzul
Art Producer: Sue Bischofberger
Editor: Eliza Kirby
Production Editor: Mia Moran
Production Manager: Jose Olivera
Illustrations © 2021 Lucy Kirk

ISBN: Print 978-1-64876-941-2
R0

This Journal Belongs to:

"[Gratitude] turns what we have into enough, and more. It turns denial into acceptance, chaos into order, confusion into clarity . . . Gratitude makes sense of our past, brings peace for today, and creates a vision for tomorrow."

—MELODY BEATTIE

CONTENTS

Introduction **vi**

I am so glad to be able to share this gratitude journal with you. No matter who you are or what is going on in your life, gratitude can help you live life more fully, in small and big ways.

I have long practiced being thankful for all the good things in my life each night when I go to bed. This simple routine helps me remember that no matter how my day went, I have so much to be grateful for. In this small, everyday way, it makes it easier for me to relax and fall asleep.

The true power of gratitude became clearest to me when I faced my biggest challenges. When I lost someone I loved, I found comfort in being grateful for the people I still had in my life. When I felt something unfair messed up the plans I had for my future, I found strength in being grateful for my ability to start from scratch and create new possibilities.

You may think that gratitude is something that only rich people or happy people can feel. However, gratitude can actually be just as powerful and heartfelt when you are at your lowest moments. In fact, gratitude can help you most when you're not feeling your best. It helps you look up and see the beauty that is out there, even if it seems like nothing is going right.

I hope this gratitude journal helps you develop the everyday habit of gratitude so that you can use it as a strength when you come up against the big obstacles in life.

What Is Gratitude?

Gratitude is all about being thankful. Each of us has so much to be grateful for, from little things like the air we breathe to big things like a safe roof over our head. When we take time to practice gratitude, we focus on and give importance to the good things in our lives. As you work through this book's prompts and exercises, you may notice yourself feeling more positive. Even small exercises of gratitude can amount to a big perspective change. In fact, studies have connected gratitude to higher levels of happiness, improved resilience, and even improved academic performance.

The best way to get the most from your gratitude practice is to develop a daily habit. In this way, you will learn to naturally incorporate gratitude into your life—it'll become a part of your everyday routine. Gratitude can help you find strength when you encounter hardships. If you practice it every day, it will be there to support you when you need it most.

How to Use This Book

This book includes a recurring element to check in with your feelings and quick habit-forming opportunities to express what you are grateful for each day. It also contains prompts to cultivate greater awareness of your surroundings and deeper gratitude for yourself, others, and your life at large. Interspersed with these prompts, you'll find inspiring quotes and some exercises to deepen your gratitude practice.

While this journal will help you deepen your experience with gratitude, it is not a replacement for a therapist, medication, or medical treatment. There is no shame in seeking help when life gets to be too stressful. I hope you enjoy this guided journal and feel a little happier after each exercise! Take joy in each writing prompt, knowing that you are doing this for *you*.

A New Lens

The way we experience life is often affected by the lens through which we see it. Gratitude is all about a subtle but powerful perspective shift. Where things may have seemed unfocused and fuzzy before, a lens of gratitude can help us see more clearly what is important. The following prompts, exercises, and quotes will help you notice things in your life and look at them in a new way. You are beginning the journey of awareness and appreciation. It is amazing how a small shift toward an attitude of gratitude can have a huge impact on how you feel and how you interact with the world around you. You may notice that when you feel happier, you produce better results for yourself, both in your relationships and in reaching your goals.

I awoke this morning with devout thanksgiving for my friends, the old and the new.

—RALPH WALDO EMERSON

Today, I am grateful for

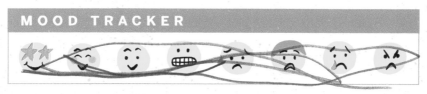

It's easy to get lost in the habit of your morning routine, but each morning holds so much to be thankful for. Think about everything you do, no matter how small, to get ready to leave the house. What are some things you encounter every morning that you're glad you have? How do they make your day better?

I am gratfull for my
PHONE

Today, I am grateful for

Nature is full of jaw-dropping beauty like waterfalls and everyday delights like flowers. Have you ever stopped to think about how much the universe provides for us? When you slow down and look around at the natural world, what are 5 to 10 things you are grateful for?

- Mom
- Dad
- Jinoses
- framly
- bomp
- bison
- Nene
- pop

Today, I am grateful for

School teaches you useful things like how to read. What skills have you learned at school that you're glad you have? They don't even have to be academic.

Today, I am grateful for _____

Reflect on something nice that an adult in your life did for you recently. What did they do? Did they have to do it? Why did they do it? Did you enjoy it? Did you let them know you thought it was nice?

_____

_____

_____

_____

_____

_____

_____

_____

_____

_____

_____

_____

Think of your favorite food.

Think about all the people who worked to grow that food, transport that food, sell that food, buy that food, and prepare that food. Imagine all the effort and time that go into your favorite food to make it available for you. Take a few moments to send gratitude to everyone who contributed toward the food you eat by imagining thanking each person for their part in the process.

Today, I am grateful for _____

Our health is often something that is easy to take for granted when we are healthy. If our body fails us or gets sick, then we notice what a difference it makes. List 5 to 10 body parts you're grateful for, and write about what they allow you to do.

_____

_____

_____

_____

_____

_____

_____

_____

_____

_____

_____

_____

"In ordinary life, we hardly realize that we receive a great deal more than we give, and that it is only with gratitude that life becomes rich.

—DIETRICH BONHOEFFER

Today, I am grateful for _____

Who was the last person you thanked? What did you thank them for? If you could tell anyone (dead or alive, anywhere in the world) that you are thankful for them, who would it be and why?

_____

_____

_____

_____

_____

_____

_____

_____

_____

_____

_____

_____

Today, I am grateful for

What is something you learned recently that you are glad you know? It doesn't have to be something you learned in school. How can you use this information in your daily life? Is there anyone you think would find this information interesting or valuable?

Today, I am grateful for _____

Sometimes we take people for granted. When we stop and remember how special our relationship with each person is, it can be inspiring. Name someone in your life who you are thankful for. How does that person make you feel? What do they do to let you know how much they care for you? What are qualities that you admire in that person? Do they know how you feel?

Dance to your favorite song.

Notice how it feels to enjoy the music and move your body. You may want to work this into your schedule more often. Sometimes gratitude can make us feel joyous, and sometimes joy can make us feel grateful!

Today, I am grateful for _____

What changes about your attitude when you get a good night's sleep? Next time you wake up feeling particularly well rested, write about it here.

_____

_____

_____

_____

_____

_____

_____

_____

_____

_____

_____

_____

_____

Today, I am grateful for _____

Consider the movements you make throughout your day, from texting and typing to drama class or an after-school sport. Make a list of five different ways you move your body. Can you find gratitude in each of these movements?

Today, I am grateful for _____

Name one friend you are grateful for. This can be a person your age, a pet, or a relative. It's okay to think outside the box. How has this friend made you feel special? What are your favorite qualities in this friend?

_____

_____

_____

_____

_____

_____

_____

_____

_____

_____

_____

_____

Today, I am grateful for

MOOD TRACKER

Even failure is something to be thankful for because it means you chose to try and it provides the opportunity to learn. Name one thing that you failed at. What did you learn from the experience?

Today, I am grateful for _____

Have you ever felt like someone was nagging you or expecting too much of you? Think about the intentions behind those actions. Even if these expectations felt like too much in the moment, did you learn something from the experience?

Try a visualization exercise.

Set a timer for 10 minutes, and sit somewhere safe and comfortable. Close your eyes. Imagine yourself all alone in an empty space. Think about all the things in your life that you have to be grateful for, and visualize them next to you. You will begin filling all the empty space around you with the things and people that make your life better.

Today, I am grateful for _____

Even the weather is something we can be thankful for. Variety in itself is something to enjoy. What's your favorite kind of weather? List a few types of weather and how they benefit you and the world around you.

_____

_____

_____

_____

_____

_____

_____

_____

_____

_____

_____

_____

_____

When we give cheerfully and accept gratefully, everyone is blessed.

—MAYA ANGELOU

Today, I am grateful for _____

What subjects do you enjoy learning about? What's the best way for you to learn new information? Do you have certain teachers or classmates who make the experience more fun?

Today, I am grateful for

Sometimes the really basic things are the most important and the easiest to take for granted. For example: water. Why do you appreciate water? List everything you use water for in your daily life.

Today, I am grateful for _____

Think of all the different types of relationships you have and how each one gives you something to be thankful for. Try listing 10 people (family, friends, teachers, etc.) who you're happy to have in your life. Most often our gratitude will be for the good things they do or say. Sometimes our gratitude may be for lessons they teach us, even if we're learning from their mistakes.

Treat yourself to a gratitude walk. Set a timer for 10 minutes, and walk in a place you feel safe and comfortable. This might be your neighborhood, a park, or anyplace you can walk freely. Notice the sounds, smells, sights. Do you see any animals? Do you hear cars or kids? Do you feel the sun or a breeze? See if you can find three things to be thankful for while on your walk.

Today, I am grateful for _____

It's easy to lose sight of gratitude when we compare ourselves to others, especially when it comes to our physical selves. Why can't we be as strong or fast as that person? Try reframing thoughts like those with gratitude in your heart for what you do have. Make a list of all the things your body does for you that you're grateful for and couldn't live without.

_____

_____

_____

_____

_____

_____

_____

_____

_____

_____

Today, I am grateful for

Joy is one of the most wonderful emotions. Is there someone or something that always makes you laugh? What was the last thing that made you feel happy or joyful?

"

As we express our
gratitude, we must
never forget that the
highest appreciation is
not to utter words, but
to live by them.

—JOHN F. KENNEDY

"

Today, I am grateful for

We are fortunate to be able to do fun things, whether it's spending time with a relative or spending time outside. What are some activities you are thankful you get to do just because they're fun? What do you enjoy about each thing?

Today, I am grateful for _____

Do you have a favorite place where you enjoy going to be alone or to feel comfortable and relax? List your favorite things about your favorite places that you are grateful for.

_____

_____

_____

_____

_____

_____

_____

_____

_____

_____

_____

Today, I am grateful for

Being able to buy things is a wonderful privilege. Receiving gifts is a lovely compliment. It is nice to have things of your own. What is one of your favorite possessions? How did you come to have it? What do you enjoy about it?

Today, I am grateful for _____

Sometimes the very same things that cause us fear or anxiety can actually give us joy if we look at them in a new way. Try listing something that gives you discomfort and see if you can find a positive way to look at it. For example, the future may scare you because it is so wide open and undefined. Or you can be thankful that it is not already written in stone and you can change your mind as you go.

_____

_____

_____

_____

_____

_____

_____

_____

Enjoy a meditation. Set a timer for 10 minutes, and sit somewhere safe and comfortable. Close your eyes, and slow your breathing. Take several deep breaths in and out. As you breathe out, release any anxiety or worries. As you breathe in, think of all that your body does that you are thankful for. Relax and feel gratitude for your body, which allows you to live.

Today, I am grateful for _____

What are you good at doing? What are you getting better at doing? List some of your talents and abilities. Who believed in you and encouraged you along the way? Who taught you things you wanted to learn? Who inspires you to keep improving?

2

The Stories I Tell Myself

The stories we tell ourselves (about ourselves and the world around us) affect the way we feel and behave. Negative thought patterns can get in our way and make it hard to achieve our goals. While gratitude is often an external practice ("I am grateful for my mom, dog, teacher, etc."), it is also important to express gratitude for yourself ("I am grateful for my ability to learn and improve"). Just as gratitude can be a useful lens for viewing the world and determining what is truly important, it can also help us create healthy inner narratives about ourselves. Improving your relationship to gratitude will allow you to have more positive feelings about yourself and the world around you.

"The heart that gives thanks is a happy one, for we cannot feel thankful and unhappy at the same time.

—DOUGLAS WOOD

Today, I am grateful for

Choosing to turn gratitude upon yourself does not mean that you are being arrogant or conceited. Being thankful for your own talents and abilities does not lessen your thankfulness for the talents and abilities of others. In fact, it would be hard to truly practice gratitude toward others if you did not know how to feel grateful for yourself. So go ahead and give yourself permission to be grateful for all that you are! Remember that gratitude does not require perfection. List 5 things about yourself for which you feel gratitude.

Today, I am grateful for _____

What are some negative thoughts that keep you from being more confident? Write them down. Now take a moment to really think about what you wrote. Just because you have a thought does not make it true. Where did that negative story come from?

_____

_____

_____

_____

_____

_____

_____

_____

_____

_____

_____

Today, I am grateful for

Try to reframe the negative thoughts you listed in the last prompt in a positive way. For example, one negative thought might be "I'm so stupid." Maybe some other kid told you that, or maybe you noticed you didn't learn something as fast as someone else. Either way, it doesn't make that thought true, and you can choose to let it go. You might reframe that thought by thinking, "I am grateful that I can learn and improve at my own speed."

Sometimes you may feel that something is blocking your gratitude. It is important to examine your feelings. If you keep replaying hurtful words or a situation that felt unfair, it can stop you from being positive. It is important to be able to set the past aside and focus on the current moment. You can't change something that happened in the past, but you can focus on being grateful that you can shape the present by choosing your current thoughts and actions. You can't control the future, but you can control what you do and say right now. Is there something you want to let go of? Think about it for a while. When you are ready, say this out loud: "I let go of my anger about the past and my worry about the future. I choose to focus on the present. I am grateful to be able to shape the moment that I am in." Pause and say it again until you feel like you really mean it.

Today, I am grateful for

Take one of the personality traits you are thankful for and share a story about a time when that trait really worked out well for you. It may be a story about a time when something almost went wrong but that trait helped solve a problem or make some-one happy.

Today, I am grateful for _____

Every person has different experiences and different abilities. Sometimes things come more easily to one person than to another. Either way, there is much to be grateful for, whether it is a natural talent or the ability to work hard and persevere. What are some abilities you have that you are thankful for and why?

_____

_____

_____

_____

_____

_____

_____

_____

_____

_____

_____

_____

We can only be said
to be alive in those
moments when our hearts
are conscious of our
treasures.

—THORNTON WILDER

Today, I am grateful for _____

It's easy to judge ourselves harshly for our failures, but we can also choose to be grateful for the chance to learn. Can you think of a time when you felt guilt or shame for something you wish you had done differently? Did you learn something valuable from the experience? What was it? Will you do better next time?

Today, I am grateful for

Sometimes the relationship we have with our parents or other adults in our lives can be difficult. Can you reframe how you think about those relationships with gratitude? For example, maybe you think, "My parents are always on my case." One way to reframe this would be "I am grateful that my parents love me and care enough to try to help me make good decisions."

Today, I am grateful for _____

Each of our weaknesses is an opportunity to grow and develop. How are you different now than you were one year ago? What are some ways in which you have changed as a person that you are grateful for?

_____

_____

_____

_____

_____

_____

_____

_____

_____

_____

_____

_____

Our bodies do so much for us every day. It's easy to take them for granted. What's your favorite exercise, physical activity, or hobby? Set some time aside to do one of your favorite activities. It could be something as simple as a walk or even just stretching. Think about how your body helps you as you do these things.

Today, I am grateful for _____

Have you ever had conflict or difficulty with a friend? Is there a way to look back at that experience with gratitude? Maybe you learned something about friendship or gained a new perspective.

_____

_____

_____

_____

_____

_____

_____

_____

_____

_____

_____

_____

Today, I am grateful for

Our actions say a lot about us. What do you like about the way you treat others? List some nice things you've done for others or plan to do in the future.

Today, I am grateful for _____

MOOD TRACKER

Sometimes seeing ourselves through the eyes of others can help us see new things to be thankful for. What are three positive things you think a family member would say about you?

_____

_____

_____

_____

_____

_____

_____

_____

_____

_____

_____

_____

Today, I am grateful for

Choose two friends. What are three positive things you think each of your friends would say about you? Are they the same things or different things?

Today, I am grateful for _____

All of us get to make at least some small choices for ourselves. What are some freedoms you are grateful for?

_____

_____

_____

_____

_____

_____

_____

_____

_____

_____

_____

_____

_____

_____

_____

_____

_____

It is good to be able to express self-appreciation freely. Look at yourself in the mirror while you express gratitude for two things you like about your appearance. Do this until it feels natural. Now look at yourself in the mirror while you express gratitude for two things you like about your personality. Repeat this until it feels natural. Did both come easily? Was one harder than the other?

Today, I am grateful for _____

Different people notice different things about us. What are three positive things you think your teachers would say about you?

We take for granted the very things that most deserve our gratitude.

—CYNTHIA OZICK

Today, I am grateful for _____

Each of us takes pleasure in different things. What are some things you get to do that you enjoy and would like to express gratitude for?

_____

_____

_____

_____

_____

_____

_____

_____

_____

_____

Today, I am grateful for

Chances are your family isn't perfect. Most families aren't. However, there is still a lot to be grateful for. What are some things about your family you are grateful for?

Today, I am grateful for _____

Who was the first friend you remember making? Are you still friends? What did they teach you about friendship that you are grateful to have learned?

Choose a friend or a family member who you are thankful for. Think about why you are thankful for them. What do they do for you? What do they say that makes you feel good? What makes you feel grateful about your relationship with that person? Then go tell them! Don't just feel gratitude—express it out loud. You'll be surprised how good expressing gratitude can make you feel.

Today, I am grateful for _____

MOOD TRACKER

See if you can fill this page with a list of all the simple things you often take for granted but today you wish to express gratitude for.

_____

_____

_____

_____

_____

_____

_____

_____

_____

_____

_____

_____

_____

_____

Today, I am grateful for

Express your gratitude for the leisure time you get. List all the different ways in which you get to enjoy your free time.

Gratitude is a powerful catalyst for happiness. It's the spark that lights a fire of joy in your soul.

—AMY COLLETTE

Today, I am grateful for

School isn't always easy or fun, but it's an opportunity to learn skills you'll use later, from academic skills to social skills to life lessons. You might be surprised by what ends up being useful. What's something you've learned at school that you ended up using in real life?

Today, I am grateful for _____

Each one of us is unique. What are some of your own qualities that you don't see in people around you?

_____

_____

_____

_____

_____

_____

_____

_____

_____

_____

_____

_____

Today, I am grateful for

What do you like about your family? List one quality about each family member for which you would like to express gratitude.

Today, I am grateful for _____

MOOD TRACKER

Worrying too much can really drain your energy. You may find it helpful to try shifting your mindset from worried to grateful. Often we can actually feel grateful for the things we are worried about. For example, if you tend to spend lots of time worrying about whether people enjoy your company, you can be grateful that you care about other people's feelings. What is something you have been overthinking lately? How can you be grateful instead?

Choose a teacher, friend, or pet that you're grateful to have in your life. Show them your gratitude by doing something nice for them. You get to be creative when you pick what you will do. It should be a small action but something that shows you care. Bake them some treats, buy or make a card, or just help out with an errand. The choice is yours.

Today, I am grateful for _____

Each of us has a different personality. We each have our own way of thinking about the world and handling challenges. What are some of your own personality traits for which you are thankful and why?

_____

_____

_____

_____

_____

_____

_____

_____

_____

_____

_____

_____

_____

A Tool for the Tough Stuff

Being a teenager is notoriously full of difficult emotions and challenges. The ability to find gratitude in the midst of the tough stuff can help you overcome and rise above.

When things are at their worst, being grateful may not come naturally. However, gratitude is not about denying or ignoring what is wrong. Instead, it is about finding moments of peace even when you are in the midst of a challenging time. It is also about reframing experiences and finding opportunities for learning.

We can all get overwhelmed by negative situations. Gratitude can help you find the strength and perspective to move past the emotions that can feel overwhelming.

"

I would maintain
that thanks are the
highest form of thought;
and that gratitude
is happiness doubled
by wonder.

—G.K. CHESTERTON

"

Today, I am grateful for

Gratitude can help you learn to deal with minor unpleasant emotions and help you turn a negative outlook into a more positive one. For example, maybe you felt annoyed because someone asked you a favor, and you felt it gave you less free time. But maybe doing the favor gave you a chance to connect on a deeper level with that person. What is a minor unpleasant emotion you have dealt with recently? Can you find anything in the situation to be grateful about?

Today, I am grateful for _____

Often when we are facing a huge challenge, we might not feel grateful. Negative emotions may take over. In those situations, finding gratitude in simple things can help transition your focus. Maybe you notice the way the sun warms your back. Focus on being grateful for that warm feeling. Can you think of a time when you felt gratitude for something small and it helped you through a tough experience?

Today, I am grateful for

Can you think of a situation where you felt jealousy? Instead of reliving the event and feeling all of those old feelings, ask yourself what you feel grateful for now that it's over. Maybe you were able to grow as a person or learn something about yourself or someone else. Can you find ways to be thankful for this situation even though you may not have been at the time?

Today, I am grateful for _____

Sometimes unpleasant emotions are alerting us to something worthy of our attention. For example, if you fear public speaking, you might ask yourself why. The fear is letting you know what you can practice to improve your skills. Can you think of a fear that provides you with an opportunity to be grateful?

Our emotions are important.

Learning to understand what we are feeling and why we are feeling that way is the basis for being able to shift our perspective. Set a timer and sit in a safe, quiet place with your eyes closed for 10 minutes. Relax and examine your feelings. If you experience any uncomfortable emotions, such as anxiety, sadness, anger, or jealousy, try to see if it is possible for you to shift your perspective and focus on gratitude. For example, if you are feeling anxious about schoolwork, you might recognize that this is a natural response and then choose to focus on feeling thankful that you get to attend school or that you have a teacher you like or a favorite class. While thinking about all the things you are grateful for, you may find that your mood feels more positive.

Today, I am grateful for _____

Can you think of a time recently when you felt angry? Acknowledge that feeling, but do not give in to it. Instead, ask yourself if there is something that came out of that situation for which you can now feel grateful. Did the experience teach you something? Did it draw out of you a new response or ability?

> Cultivate the habit of being grateful for every good thing that comes to you, and to give thanks continuously. And because all things have contributed to your advancement, you should include all things in your gratitude.

—WALLACE D. WATTLES

Today, I am grateful for _____

Looking for an opportunity to feel gratitude can help us make painful experiences more bearable. Did someone recently hurt your feelings? Maybe it was a small thing they said or did. Think of how you reacted. Is there something about the way you handled the situation that you can feel grateful for? Maybe you learned how to stand up for yourself or to let little things slide. Maybe it came out better than it could have. What about that situation can you be thankful for?

_____

_____

_____

_____

_____

_____

_____

_____

_____

_____

Today, I am grateful for

Gratitude is an excellent tool for getting through rough times. However, we can often develop gratitude and feel it more easily when we're dealing with small, everyday problems. Was there a small incident today that you can turn toward gratitude? Perhaps you already did. Write about that here.

Today, I am grateful for _____

We all experience stress at some point, whether it is from school, friends, or family. Sometimes it can even be stressful just trying to live up to our own expectations. Acknowledge this feeling, and then see how you can pivot your awareness to gratitude. What are some things that help calm you and make you feel happy when you're stressed?

Today, I am grateful for

Think of a relationship that you have had with someone that you no longer have. Maybe it's an old friend you've lost touch with, or maybe it's a loved one who has left this world. Sometimes even sad, painful things have a lot of lessons to teach us or memories to be grateful for. Can you list some positive lessons you learned from that person or memories you still enjoy about them?

Today, I am grateful for _____

Anxiety can be a hard feeling to fight. It often causes us to replay events and wonder why they happened, if they could have happened differently, if they were our fault, or if we could have prevented them. These nagging questions don't help us if they are on constant replay. If you feel anxiety about a specific past event, acknowledge the anxiety as a reminder to do something differently next time. Write down a few lessons you are grateful you learned. If you feel a general sense of anxiety, then try listing all the things you are grateful for, big or small.

Sometimes your emotions need an outlet and being active can provide your body with a chance to blow off steam and relieve stress. Sometimes your body's activity can actually improve your mood, taking you from tired and upset to reinvigorated and refreshed. Shift your focus from negative emotions by focusing on gratitude for your body as you walk, run, dance, or otherwise be active for 30 minutes. Physical activity may help you in more ways than one.

" "

He is a wise man who does not grieve for the things which he has not, but rejoices for those which he has.

—EPICTETUS

" "

Today, I am grateful for

If you feel anxiety about something in the future, try turning negative thoughts into positive ones. For example, if you're nervous about a big test coming up, instead of "I hate studying," try "I am grateful for how much I am learning." List a few negative thoughts, and then rewrite them as positive thoughts.

Today, I am grateful for _____

In times of intense stress, instead of expecting yourself to handle everything, you may find it helpful to be grateful for your support system. Do you have a friend, adult, or counselor you can turn to for help? How have they helped you in the past?

_____

_____

_____

_____

_____

_____

_____

_____

_____

_____

_____

_____

One way to manage stress is to focus on your breathing.

Breathing exercises can increase oxygen in your bloodstream and improve your calm and focus. Sit quietly in a safe place, and practice lengthening your breaths. Take a deep breath in through your nose, and then breathe out slowly through your mouth. Pause and repeat over and over. Imagine yourself breathing in gratitude and breathing out your negative emotions. You may find it helpful to say in your mind, "I breathe in a spirit of gratitude" as you breathe in and "I breathe out anxiety and release it" as you breathe out. Breathing in and out deeply can help center you and allow you to refocus.

Today, I am grateful for _____

While it is normal and natural to feel sadness when something goes wrong, you don't want to get stuck in your sadness. What is a small incident that made you feel sad recently? Can you think of some ways to feel grateful about this incident now that it is over?

Today, I am grateful for

Can you recall a time when you had a fight with a friend? What negative emotions did that cause? How did you get past those negative feelings? What did you learn from the fight? Is there something about the experience for which you can feel grateful?

Today, I am grateful for _____

Think of a situation where you felt like you did something wrong. It's easy to think of what you could have done better, but what if you thought about how things could have gone worse? This may help you recognize that the situation isn't as disastrous as you thought it was. Did your negative feelings from that experience prevent you from having positive emotions or experiencing gratitude? Has answering these questions provided you a chance to change your perspective about the situation? If so, how?

That's the gift of gratitude: In order to feel it, your ego has to take a backseat.

—OPRAH WINFREY

Today, I am grateful for _____

Sometimes fear of failure is worse than the failure itself. We put pressure on ourselves to be perfect or perform well, which often makes us scared to make mistakes. Ask yourself what would happen if you failed. Would life still go on? Would there still be plenty to be thankful for? Does being relieved from some of the pressure of failure make it easier to perform?

Today, I am grateful for

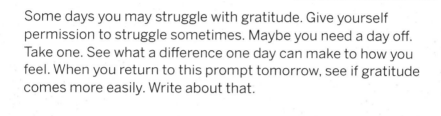

Some days you may struggle with gratitude. Give yourself permission to struggle sometimes. Maybe you need a day off. Take one. See what a difference one day can make to how you feel. When you return to this prompt tomorrow, see if gratitude comes more easily. Write about that.

Today, I am grateful for _____

Do you catch yourself feeling jealous of other people? While that is a natural, normal feeling, it can fester into something unhealthy. Instead, try using your attitude of gratitude and be thankful that they have so much, that the universe has so much, and that there is plenty for everyone. Think of a specific time you have noticed yourself feeling jealous lately. How can you shift your perspective?

_____

_____

_____

_____

_____

_____

_____

_____

_____

_____

Today, I am grateful for

Do you ever feel deep-rooted anger about something that happened in the past? These strong emotions may be letting you know that something is unresolved. It is likely you still have a lesson to learn. Can you try reframing the past? It's okay to still feel angry, but is there something about the situation for which you can be thankful?

Today, I am grateful for _____

When something goes wrong, you might find yourself placing blame on other people. When you feel overwhelmed by negative emotions toward another person, it helps to think about empathy. Can you think of a situation recently when you blamed someone else? Try to put yourself in the other person's shoes. Can you imagine how they might be feeling or why they may have responded the way they did?

Think of someone who recently listened to you when you were going through a hard time and needed to vent or someone who gave you excellent advice. Seek them out and let them know how much it meant to you or how much it helped you. You may be surprised that sharing your gratitude will make not only them feel good but you, too!

At times, our own light goes out and is rekindled by a spark from another person. Each of us has cause to think with deep gratitude of those who have lighted the flame within us.

—ALBERT SCHWEITZER

Today, I am grateful for

Negative emotions don't always have an obvious outside source. Sometimes it is our own comparison or expectations that make us feel down. It's not always easy, but it helps to practice self-gratitude and self-love. List the ways in which you deserve some acknowledgment for the good things you do. Give yourself credit for the efforts you are making and the goals you have reached.

Today, I am grateful for

Sometimes you may feel depressed or upset and not know why. But think about this: You have a lot of growth happening in your body and in your mind. That all takes a lot of energy, and it can make everything else feel more difficult. List the ways in which you are growing and changing. Can you find something to be grateful about for each of these changes?

Today, I am grateful for

Can you recall an experience of negative peer pressure? How about an experience with positive peer pressure? What can you now find to be grateful for from those situations?

Today, I am grateful for _____

Being betrayed, disappointed, or hurt is never easy. It may cause you to feel angry or sad or confused. Sometimes we carry big hurts around with us for a long time. While reliving old hurts is not helpful, reframing them can be. Maybe you can find a way to be grateful for the experience because it helped make you who you are today. Are you stronger than you thought? Do you give yourself credit for finding forgiveness or overcoming a challenging situation?

One of the deepest forms of wisdom comes from intuition, which is often felt from the heart. Try to listen hard to your heart. Do you hear its beats? What do they tell you? If we cultivate gratitude for the heart—its wants or its beats—we get better at listening to ourselves, understanding the needs of others, and finding a way to achieve our goals. What is your heart telling you?

Today, I am grateful for _____

What negative emotion do you struggle with most? What is that emotion trying to tell you? Does it teach you something?

_____

_____

_____

_____

_____

_____

_____

_____

_____

_____

_____

_____

_____

Thanks, World

Your gratitude journey is about taking time to be more observant and in the moment. We have seen how being grateful can cause a beautiful shift in perspective within our immediate circles and with our image of ourselves. We have even gotten a glimpse of how gratitude can help us in times of crisis. This section invites you to expand your sense of thankfulness to include the world at large. These exercises and prompts will help cultivate a sense of graciousness toward new people, new places, animals, plants, and your areas of interest—there are no limits or rules when it comes to gratitude.

Today, I am grateful for _____

MOOD TRACKER

Think of the world at large and list 5 to 10 things you are grateful for. Try to expand your thinking beyond your family, friends, and immediate surroundings. Anything in the universe qualifies. What do you appreciate about these things?

Today, I am grateful for _____

Often, people we don't know can have an impact on our lives. It can be as tiny as the person who decides to pick up a nail on the road instead of just walking past it. They may prevent you from getting a flat tire and allow you to get somewhere important on time. Can you find gratitude for people who do the right thing even though others may never get to see them do it? Think of a specific person or a specific action for which you would like to express your thanks, and do so here.

> # I don't have to chase extraordinary moments to find happiness—it's right in front of me if I'm paying attention and practicing gratitude.
>
> —BRENÉ BROWN

Today, I am grateful for

List three of your favorite animals that you have seen and three you'd like to see someday. Is there something about animals that you can be grateful for?

Today, I am grateful for _____

What are some of your main areas of interest right now? How do you learn more about those subjects? Do you think these will still be on the top of your list a few years from now? Has answering these questions made you feel grateful for anything? Share that here.

_____

_____

_____

_____

_____

_____

_____

_____

_____

_____

_____

Today, I am grateful for _____

Think about how big our world is. We can never explore it all, but it includes so many amazing things, from nature to diverse cultures. Does this make you feel grateful for anything?

Today, I am grateful for _____

Take a moment to look around. List three to five things in your surroundings that you are thankful for. Why do you appreciate these particular items?

_____

_____

_____

_____

_____

_____

_____

_____

_____

_____

_____

_____

_____

> **Gratitude goes beyond the 'mine' and 'thine' and claims the truth that all of life is a pure gift.**
>
> —HENRI NOUWEN

Today, I am grateful for _____

Have you ever met a person who taught you something new or helped you see things in a different way? What new thought or perception are you grateful to have been exposed to?

_____

_____

_____

_____

_____

_____

_____

_____

_____

_____

_____

_____

_____

Make a special effort to thank someone each day. One day you might thank your sibling for letting you have the remote. Another day you might thank your friend for their great advice. You may even decide to thank a parent for reminding you to do your homework!

Today, I am grateful for

The opportunity to learn is something we can take advantage of our entire lives, even after we finish school. Our exposures to different people, places, cultures, subjects, and experiences give us the chance to grow and change. In what ways have you already grown and changed?

Today, I am grateful for

Do you like to daydream? What do you appreciate about it? How does it make you feel?

Today, I am grateful for _____

It is never too late to try new things. What's something you've never done that you might like to pursue someday? Maybe you might like to try gardening or play an instrument, for example. When thinking about this, what are you most grateful for?

_____

_____

_____

_____

_____

_____

_____

_____

_____

_____

_____

_____

Sometimes we don't take the time to fully appreciate our surroundings. Plants often fall into that category. Take a walk and take the time to really look at the plants you see on your walk. Notice their colors, shapes, sizes, and textures. Notice if you pass an area without any plants, and realize how much they impact your enjoyment of what you see. Do any of the plants you pass provide food for people or other animals? Take note of how many different kinds of plants you see. Allow yourself to feel grateful for the variety, number, and many uses of plants.

Today, I am grateful for _____

Can you think of three to five places you would like to explore someday? What about those places do you find interesting? Do you enjoy having something to look forward to exploring?

Today, I am grateful for

Many of us grow up seeing only one type of landscape on a regular basis. However, getting a chance to see a new type of terrain, either in person or in a video, can be quite an experience. What do you appreciate about the landscape around you? What natural elements in other areas are you most grateful for?

"When I started counting my blessings, my whole life turned around.

-WILLIE NELSON

Today, I am grateful for

Sometimes looking at similarities and differences can help us be grateful for things we hadn't noticed before. Compare and contrast two things of importance in your life. For example, you might compare and contrast where you live now with some-where you'd like to live in the future. What can you find to be grateful for in each situation?

Today, I am grateful for _____

Sometimes people we've never even met in real life can still be an inspiration to us. Who is a person that you find inspiring? Why are you grateful for their example? What do they make you want to do, think, or accomplish?

Today, I am grateful for

What are some sounds you are thankful for? It could be the sound a basketball makes as it goes through the hoop. It could be the sound of plates being set out on the table. The options are endless.

Today, I am grateful for _____

Scents can be enjoyable simply for what they are or for things they remind us of. What are some smells you are grateful for? Maybe it's the scent of popcorn popping or the smell of grass just after it has been cut.

Our connections with people are great ways to learn more about the world and to enjoy ourselves. Are you open to meeting new people and learning things? When you are in a safe environment, like school, seek out the opportunity to get to know someone new. You might try things like saying hello to the librarian, offering to show a new kid around, or volunteering to visit an elderly neighbor. Engaging in new conversations can be a great way to learn. You might even try interacting with people like your grandparents in a new way and make the conversation about them. Find out how life was different for them growing up or how they chose their career. We can learn all kinds of new things if we engage and connect with others.

Today, I am grateful for _____

MOOD TRACKER

List three to five sensations you are thankful for. It might be the feel of warmth on your skin when you sit by a fire or jumping in a cold pool on a hot day.

_____

_____

_____

_____

_____

_____

_____

_____

_____

_____

_____

_____

Gratitude is a divine emotion: it fills the heart, but not to bursting; it warms it, but not to fever.

—CHARLOTTE BRONTË

Today, I am grateful for _____

Share a memory about a time you spent in nature that you're grateful for. Maybe it was a day at the beach, a walk in the park, or sitting in your backyard. What did you see? How did you interact with your surroundings? How did the place make you feel?

Today, I am grateful for

List five different things that the earth provides for you to eat.
Think about how a tiny seed can grow into nourishing food. Have
you ever picked food yourself, or would you like to? How does
that make you feel grateful?

Today, I am grateful for _____

Share a vivid image of something that makes you feel happy and free. Think about how your senses felt at the time—for example, a cool breeze on a hot, sticky day or the soft fur of a pet on your skin. Write about this in as much detail as you can.

_____

_____

_____

_____

_____

_____

_____

_____

_____

_____

_____

_____

Today, I am grateful for _____

Doing something for the first time can be a milestone and an opportunity to learn and test yourself. There are so many firsts to enjoy. Can you recall something that you recently did for the first time? It can be big or small. What was it? How did it make you feel?

Today, I am grateful for _____

Each community has its own unique characteristics. You've probably noticed what makes your own area special, but can you widen your scope to feel grateful for things outside your immediate community? Name some people, things, or places that are different from where you live that you are grateful for.

_____

_____

_____

_____

_____

_____

_____

_____

_____

_____

_____

_____

This exercise will give you a visual aid of all the things you have to be thankful for. Take a poster board or a sheet of paper and decorate it with things for which you feel gratitude. A few suggestions include photos of your family, pets, and friends. You might also use drawings of things you enjoy or mementos from events that were important to you. You can use magazine photos to show things you are thankful for, like the ocean or a good meal. Use your creativity to capture your gratitude. This poster can be displayed on your wall or pulled out when you need a pick-me-up.

Today, I am grateful for _____

Think of things that you are glad exist even though you may never see them in person. What do you choose to feel grateful for right now?

_____

_____

_____

_____

_____

_____

_____

_____

_____

_____

_____

_____

Today, I am grateful for

Gratitude can show up in places you might not expect it, even if it's tiny. Can you share a bug that you feel thankful for? What do you like about it, or what good does it do?

Today, I am grateful for _____

There are lots of mysteries in the universe. What is a mystery you are thankful for? It could be something as simple as "Why do we sleep?" or as deep as "Why do we exist?" Are you grateful for the chance to ponder that mystery?

Create a daily time to express your gratitude. I do it each night before I go to sleep. You may prefer to do it each day before you get out of bed or before breakfast. What matters is creating a routine where you feel comfortable and have time to express gratitude for all the good in your life. You may prefer to do this verbally in your head or to write it down.

Gratefulness.org

A personal story of grateful living, which includes lots of information on gratitude practices and ideas.

GratitudeHabitat.com

A gratitude blog full of fresh inspiration to keep you centered on being thankful.

The 7 Habits of Highly Effective Teens, by Sean Covey

A helpful guide to improving self-image and achieving goals.

Unbroken (The Young Adult Adaptation), by Laura Hillenbrand

This powerful, true-life story is inspiring.

You Can Heal Your Life, by Louise Hay

I discovered this book as a teen and found it very helpful in facing challenges and staying positive.

ABOUT THE AUTHOR

Scarlet Paolicchi lives in Nashville, Tennessee, where she enjoys the perfect combination of city life and access to the great outdoors. After a career in retail management, she founded *Family Focus Blog*, where for a decade she has shared all things family related, from parenting advice and family dinner recipes to eco-living and travel tips. She is the wife to her Tulane University college sweetheart and mother to their two wonderful children. Her first two books were *Welcome to the Family! A Celebratory Journal for a New Big Sister or Brother* and *Sharing Stories, Making Memories: A Journal for Grandparents and Grandchildren.* You can connect with her on Facebook or Instagram @FamilyFocusBlog and read more of her writing at FamilyFocusBlog.com.

CPSIA information can be obtained
at www.ICGtesting.com
Printed in the USA
JSHW041619160721
16974JS00003B/5